MW00629484
2025

Gooseberry Patch

An imprint of Globe Pequot
64 South Main Street
Essex, CT 06426

www.gooseberrypatch.com

1•800•854•6673

Your recipe could appear in our next cookbook!

Share your tried & true family favorite recipes with us instantly at

www.gooseberrypatch.com

If you'd rather jot 'em down by hand, send them to us at:

Gooseberry Patch
Attn: Cookbook Dept.
PO Box 812
Columbus, OH 43216-0812

Don't forget to include the number of servings your recipe makes, plus your name, address, phone number and email address. If we select your recipe, your name will appear right along with it and you'll receive a **FREE** copy of the cookbook!

January

January

Write it on your heart that every day is the best day of the year.

– Ralph Waldo Emerson

Sunday	Monday	Tuesday
5	6	7
12	13	14
19	20 Martin Luther King, Jr. Day	21
26	27	28

December

S	M	T	W	T	F	S
1	2	3	4	5	6	7
8	9	10	11	12	13	14
15	16	17	18	19	20	21
22	23	24	25	26	27	28
29	30	31				

February

S	M	T	W	T	F	S
						1
2	3	4	5	6	7	8
9	10	11	12	13	14	15
16	17	18	19	20	21	22
23	24	25	26	27	28	

2025

Wednesday	Thursday	Friday	Saturday
1 New Year's Day	2	3	4
8	9	10	11
15	16	17	18
22	23	24	25
29	30	31	

January

Graham Pralines

Try these with cinnamon grahams too...yum!

1 sleeve graham crackers
1/2 c. butter
1/2 c. margarine
1 c. brown sugar, packed
1/8 t. salt
1 c. chopped pecans

Cover a baking sheet with aluminum foil; spray lightly with non-stick vegetable spray. Break crackers and arrange on baking sheet; set aside. Melt butter, margarine, sugar and salt together in a saucepan over low heat. Bring to a boil and boil for 2 minutes; pour over crackers. Sprinkle pecans over top; bake at 350 degrees for 10 to 12 minutes. Let cool; break apart. Makes about 2 dozen.

1 Wednesday New Year's Day

2 Thursday

3 Friday

4 Saturday

5 Sunday

January

Monday 6

Tuesday 7

Wednesday 8

Thursday 9

Friday 10

Saturday 11

Sunday 12

January

13 Monday

14 Tuesday

15 Wednesday

16 Thursday

17 Friday

18 Saturday

19 Sunday

January

Martin Luther King, Jr. Day

Monday 20

Tuesday 21

Wednesday 22

Thursday 23

Friday 24

Saturday 25

Sunday 26

January

27 Monday

28 Tuesday

29 Wednesday

30 Thursday

31 Friday

Keep the cheer in your home throughout the winter months by decorating with a variety of snowmen. Set them on the kitchen table, on the mantel over the fireplace and don't forget the window sills. Celebrate the snow!

February

February

Notes

January						
S	M	T	W	T	F	S
			1	2	3	4
5	6	7	8	9	10	11
12	13	14	15	16	17	18
19	20	21	22	23	24	25
26	27	28	29	30	31	

March						
S	M	T	W	T	F	S
						1
2	3	4	5	6	7	8
9	10	11	12	13	14	15
16	17	18	19	20	21	22
23/30	24/31	25	26	27	28	29

Love is an irresistible desire
to be irresistibly desired.

– Robert Frost

Sunday	Monday	Tuesday
2 Groundhog Day	3	4
9	10	11
16	17 Presidents' Day	18
23	24	25

2025

Wednesday	Thursday	Friday	Saturday
			1
5	6	7	8
12	13	14 Valentine's Day	15
19	20	21	22
26	27	28	

February

Be Mine Cherry Brownies

18.3-oz. pkg. fudge brownie mix
3 1-oz. sqs. white baking chocolate
1/3 c. whipping cream
1 c. cream cheese frosting
1/4 c. maraschino cherries, drained and chopped
1-1/2 c. semi-sweet chocolate chips
1/4 c. butter
Garnish: candy sprinkles

Prepare brownie mix according to package instructions. Line a 13"x9" baking pan with aluminum foil, leaving several inches on sides for handles. Spray bottom of foil with non-stick vegetable spray; spread batter into pan. Bake at 350 degrees for 24 to 26 minutes; let cool. Lift brownies from pan; remove foil. Use a 3-inch heart-shaped cookie cutter to cut brownies. In a microwave-safe bowl, melt white baking chocolate and whipping cream for one to 2 minutes, stirring until chocolate is melted; refrigerate 30 minutes. Stir frosting and cherries into chilled chocolate mixture; spread over brownies. In a microwave-safe bowl, melt chocolate chips and butter for one to 2 minutes, stirring until smooth. Transfer to a plastic zipping bag, snip off a tip and drizzle over brownies. Garnish with sprinkles. Makes 14.

1 Saturday

2 Sunday

Groundhog Day

February

Monday 3

Tuesday 4

Wednesday 5

Thursday 6

Friday 7

Saturday 8

Sunday 9

February

10 Monday

11 Tuesday

12 Wednesday

13 Thursday

14 Friday — Valentine's Day

15 Saturday

16 Sunday

February

Presidents' Day

Monday 17

Tuesday 18

Wednesday 19

Thursday 20

Friday 21

Saturday 22

Sunday 23

February

24 Monday

25 Tuesday

26 Wednesday

27 Thursday

28 Friday

Tell a best friend no one else can fill her shoes! Cover the lid of a plain shoe box with pictures of shoes cut from magazines or catalogs. Fill the box with homemade treats and wrap the box with pretty cotton string.

March

March

Try something new at your next girlfriends' get-together...a fabric swap! We all seem to have a stack of fabric we thought we'd use "someday," but never have, so why not share?

Sunday	Monday	Tuesday
2	3	4
9 Daylight Savings Begins	10 Commonwealth Day (Canada)	11
16	17 St. Patrick's Day	18
23 / 30	24 / 31	25

February

S	M	T	W	T	F	S
						1
2	3	4	5	6	7	8
9	10	11	12	13	14	15
16	17	18	19	20	21	22
23	24	25	26	27	28	

April

S	M	T	W	T	F	S
		1	2	3	4	5
6	7	8	9	10	11	12
13	14	15	16	17	18	19
20	21	22	23	24	25	26
27	28	29	30			

2025

Wednesday	Thursday	Friday	Saturday
			1
5 Ash Wednesday	6	7	8
12	13	14	15
19	20 First Day of Spring	21	22
26	27	28	29

March

Create a sweet mini sewing kit...it's so handy! You'll need a pint-size Mason jar with a two-part lid. Pad the flat lid piece with cotton batting, cover with a circle of fabric and slide on the jar ring. Fill the jar with needles & thread, tiny scissors and a few spare buttons, screw on the lid and it's ready to use!

1 Saturday

2 Sunday

March

Monday 3

Tuesday 4

Ash Wednesday

Wednesday 5

Thursday 6

Friday 7

Saturday 8

Daylight Savings Begins

Sunday 9

March

10 Monday

Commonwealth Day (Canada)

11 Tuesday

12 Wednesday

13 Thursday

14 Friday

15 Saturday

16 Sunday

March

St. Patrick's Day

Monday 17

Tuesday 18

Wednesday 19

First Day of Spring

Thursday 20

Friday 21

Saturday 22

Sunday 23

March

24 Monday

25 Tuesday

26 Wednesday

27 Thursday

28 Friday

29 Saturday

30 Sunday

March

Monday 

Poppy Seed Cake

The glaze drizzled over this simple cake sets it apart from other poppy seed cakes.

18-1/4 oz. pkg. yellow cake mix
1 c. oil
1 c. sour cream
1/2 c. sugar
4 eggs, beaten
1/4 c. poppy seed

In a large bowl, beat together dry cake mix and all remaining ingredients. Pour into a greased and floured Bundt® pan. Bake at 325 degrees for one hour, or until a toothpick inserted tests clean. Turn cake out onto a serving plate. Drizzle Glaze over top. Serves 8 to 10.

Glaze:

1/2 c. sugar
1/4 c. orange juice
1/2 t. almond extract
1/2 t. imitation butter flavor
1/2 t. vanilla extract

Combine all ingredients; mix well.

March

Colorful Fruit Soup

This soup is so refreshing! Freshly ground black pepper complements the sweet fruit wonderfully. Present it on a green tray for St. Patrick's Day!

1 c. seedless grapes, halved
1 c. blueberries
1/2 c. strawberries, hulled and diced
1/2 c. pineapple, peeled and diced
1/2 c. kiwi, peeled and diced
1 c. unsweetened apple juice
1/2 c. orange juice
1/4 t. pepper

Combine fruit in a large bowl. In a measuring cup, mix juices and pepper; pour over fruit mixture. Stir gently. Cover and refrigerate until serving time. Makes 6 servings.

MASON
April

April

Notes

March						
S	M	T	W	T	F	S
						1
2	3	4	5	6	7	8
9	10	11	12	13	14	15
16	17	18	19	20	21	22
23/30	24/31	25	26	27	28	29

May						
S	M	T	W	T	F	S
				1	2	3
4	5	6	7	8	9	10
11	12	13	14	15	16	17
18	19	20	21	22	23	24
25	26	27	28	29	30	31

Sunday	Monday	Tuesday
		1 April Fool's Day
6	7	8
13 Palm Sunday	14	15
20 Easter	21 Easter Monday (Canada)	22
27	28	29

2025

Wednesday	Thursday	Friday	Saturday
2	3	4	5
9	10	11	12 Passover (Sundown)
16	17	18 Good Friday	19
23	24	25	26
30			

Flowers always make people better, happier and more helpful; they are sunshine, food and medicine for the soul.

– Luther Burbank

April

1 Tuesday — April Fool's Day

2 Wednesday

3 Thursday

4 Friday

5 Saturday

6 Sunday

April

Monday 7

Tuesday 8

Wednesday 9

Thursday 10

Friday 11

Passover (Sundown)

Saturday 12

Palm Sunday

Sunday 13

April

14 Monday

15 Tuesday

16 Wednesday

17 Thursday

18 Friday

Good Friday

19 Saturday

20 Sunday

Easter

April

Easter Monday
(Canada)

Monday 21

Tuesday 22

Wednesday 23

Thursday 24

Friday 25

Saturday 26

Sunday 27

April

28 Monday

29 Tuesday

30 Wednesday

Creamsicles

Fresh orange juice makes these creamy frozen treats taste so much better than store-bought.

1 pt. vanilla ice cream or ice milk, softened
6-oz. can frozen orange juice concentrate, thawed
1/4 c. honey
1-1/2 c. fat-free milk
12 craft sticks

Combine ice cream or ice milk, orange juice concentrate and honey in a large bowl; mix well. Gradually beat in fat-free milk and pour into 12 small wax paper cups or an ice cube tray. Insert sticks into paper cups or ice cube trays when partially frozen; freeze until solid. Makes one dozen.

May

May

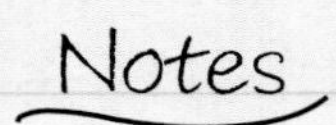

Sunday	Monday	Tuesday

A mother is she who can take the place of all others but whose place no one else can take.
– Cardinal Mermillod

4	5	6
11 Mothers' Day	12	13
18	19 Victoria Day (Canada)	20
25	26 Memorial Day	27

April

S	M	T	W	T	F	S
		1	2	3	4	5
6	7	8	9	10	11	12
13	14	15	16	17	18	19
20	21	22	23	24	25	26
27	28	29	30			

June

S	M	T	W	T	F	S
1	2	3	4	5	6	7
8	9	10	11	12	13	14
15	16	17	18	19	20	21
22	23	24	25	26	27	28
29	30					

2025

Wednesday	Thursday	Friday	Saturday
	1 May Day	2	3
7	8	9	10
14	15	16	17
21	22	23	24
28	29	30	31

May

Avocado Egg Salad Sandwiches

A fresh and delicious twist on egg salad...serve it on your favorite hearty bread!

6 eggs, hard-boiled, peeled and chopped
2 avocados, halved, pitted and cubed
1/4 c. red onion, minced
1/3 c. mayonnaise
1 T. mustard
salt and pepper to taste
12 slices thinly-sliced whole-grain bread

Mash eggs with a fork in a bowl until crumbly. Add remaining ingredients except bread slices. Gently mix together until blended. Spread egg mixture evenly over 6 bread slices. Top with remaining bread slices. Makes 6 sandwiches.

1 Thursday — May Day

2 Friday

3 Saturday

4 Sunday

May

Monday 5

Tuesday 6

Wednesday 7

Thursday 8

Friday 9

Saturday 10

Mothers' Day

Sunday 11

May

12 Monday

13 Tuesday

14 Wednesday

15 Thursday

HERBS

16 Friday

17 Saturday

18 Sunday

May

Victoria Day (Canada)

Monday 19

Tuesday 20

Wednesday 21

Thursday 22

Friday 23

Saturday 24

Sunday 25

May

26 Monday — Memorial Day

27 Tuesday

28 Wednesday

29 Thursday

30 Friday

31 Saturday

June

June

Notes

May						
S	M	T	W	T	F	S
				1	2	3
4	5	6	7	8	9	10
11	12	13	14	15	16	17
18	19	20	21	22	23	24
25	26	27	28	29	30	31

July						
S	M	T	W	T	F	S
		1	2	3	4	5
6	7	8	9	10	11	12
13	14	15	16	17	18	19
20	21	22	23	24	25	26
27	28	29	30	31		

Sunday	Monday	Tuesday
1	2	3
8	9	10
15 Fathers' Day	16	17
22	23	24
29	30	

2025

Wednesday	Thursday	Friday	Saturday
4	5	6	7
11	12	13	14 Flag Day
18	19 Juneteenth	20 First Day of Summer	21
25	26	27	28

Fried chicken is yummy cold as well as hot. Pack a picnic lunch with fried chicken, potato salad and a jug of lemonade...enjoy!

Good & Healthy "Fried" Chicken

1 c. whole-grain panko bread crumbs
1 c. cornmeal
2 T. all-purpose flour
salt and pepper to taste
10 chicken drumsticks
1 c. buttermilk

Combine panko, cornmeal, flour, salt and pepper in a gallon-size plastic zipping bag. Coat chicken with buttermilk, one piece at a time. Drop chicken into bag and shake to coat pieces lightly. Arrange chicken on a baking pan coated with non-stick vegetable spray. Bake, uncovered, at 350 degrees for 40 to 50 minutes, until chicken juices run clear. Makes 5 servings.

1 Sunday ____________________

June

Monday 2

Tuesday 3

Wednesday 4

Thursday 5

Friday 6

Saturday 7

Sunday 8

June

9 Monday

10 Tuesday

11 Wednesday

12 Thursday

13 Friday

14 Saturday — Flag Day

15 Sunday — Fathers' Day

June

Monday 16

Tuesday 17

Wednesday 18

Juneteenth

Thursday 19

First Day of Summer

Friday 20

Saturday 21

Sunday 22

June

23 Monday

24 Tuesday

25 Wednesday

26 Thursday

27 Friday

28 Saturday

29 Sunday

Banana Split Cake

2 c. graham cracker crumbs
6 T. butter, melted
2 pasteurized eggs, beaten
2 c. powdered sugar
1/4 c. margarine, softened
3 firm bananas, sliced
Optional: 1/2 c. lemon-lime soda
20-oz. can crushed pineapple, well drained
8-oz. container frozen whipped topping, thawed
6-oz. jar maraschino cherries, drained and chopped
1/2 c. chopped walnuts

In a bowl, mix together cracker crumbs and butter. Press firmly into the bottom of a 13"x9" baking pan; set aside. In another bowl, beat together eggs, powdered sugar and margarine for 5 minutes, or until smooth; spread over crumb mixture. If desired, dip banana slices into soda to prevent browning; drain. Layer banana slices over powdered sugar mixture; top with pineapple. Spread whipped topping over pineapple. Garnish with cherries; sprinkle with walnuts. Cover and refrigerate for one hour before serving. Cut into squares. Makes 10 servings.

June

Very Veggie Mac & Cheese

8-oz. pkg. whole-wheat elbow macaroni, uncooked
1 c. carrots, peeled and sliced
1 c. broccoli, chopped
1 c. cauliflower, chopped
1-1/4 c. milk
2 T. cornstarch
2 T. extra-virgin olive oil
1 red onion, chopped
4 cloves garlic, minced
1/2 c. shredded Monterey Jack cheese
1/2 c. shredded Cheddar cheese
1/4 c. cream cheese

Prepare macaroni according to package directions; add vegetables to cooking water during the last 5 minutes of cooking time. Drain; place in a serving bowl. Meanwhile, whisk together milk and cornstarch in a bowl; set aside. Heat oil in a large saucepan over medium heat. Add onion and garlic; cook, stirring frequently, for about 5 minutes. Add milk mixture to onion mixture; bring to a boil, stirring constantly. Reduce heat to low; add cheeses. Cook and stir until cheeses are melted; pour over macaroni mixture. Toss until well combined. Makes 8 servings.

July

July

Notes

June						
S	M	T	W	T	F	S
1	2	3	4	5	6	7
8	9	10	11	12	13	14
15	16	17	18	19	20	21
22	23	24	25	26	27	28
29	30					

August						
S	M	T	W	T	F	S
					1	2
3	4	5	6	7	8	9
10	11	12	13	14	15	16
17	18	19	20	21	22	23
24/31	25	26	27	28	29	30

Sunday	Monday	Tuesday
		1 Canada Day (Canada)
6	7	8
13	14	15
20	21	22
27	28	29

2025

Wednesday	Thursday	Friday	Saturday
2	3	4 Independence Day	5
9	10	11	12
16	17	18	19
23	24	25	26
30	31		

July

1 Tuesday — Canada Day (Canada)

2 Wednesday

3 Thursday

4 Friday — Independence Day

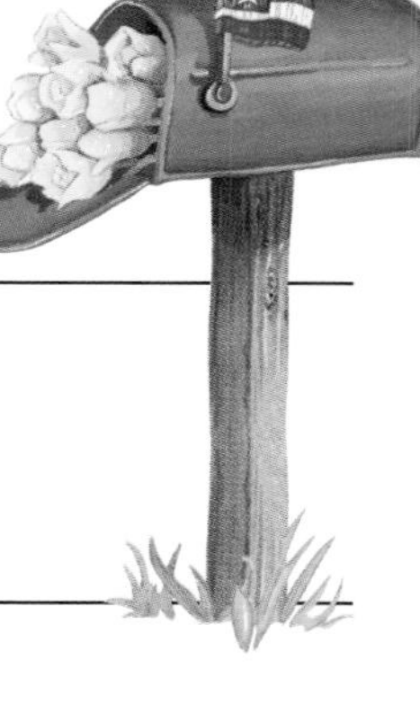

5 Saturday

6 Sunday

July

Monday 7

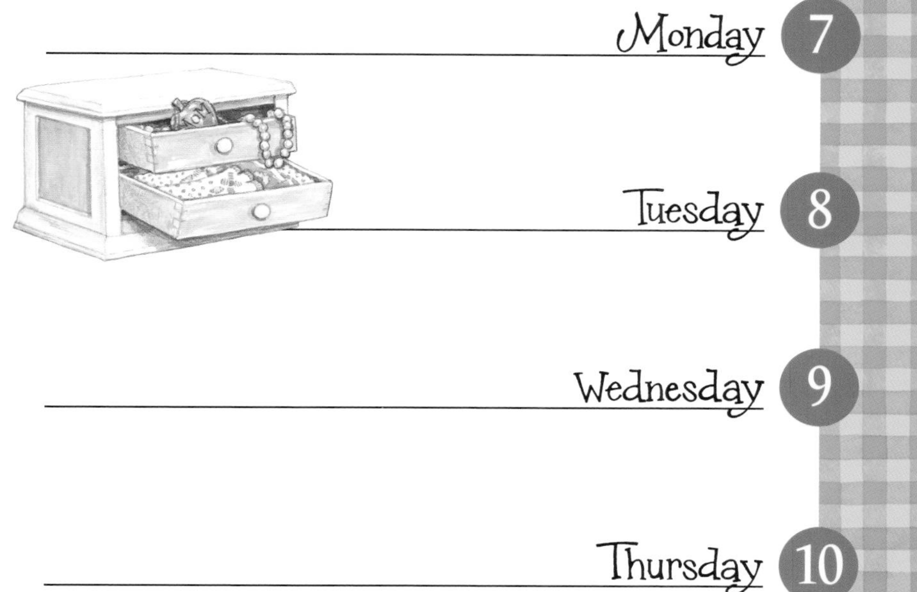

Tuesday 8

Wednesday 9

Thursday 10

Friday 11

Saturday 12

Sunday 13

July

14 Monday

15 Tuesday

16 Wednesday

17 Thursday

18 Friday

19 Saturday

20 Sunday

July

Monday 21

Tuesday 22

Wednesday 23

Thursday 24

Friday 25

Saturday 26

Sunday 27

July

28 Monday

29 Tuesday

30 Wednesday

31 Thursday

Use old serving dishes in a new way for a fresh look. Handed-down cream-and-sugar sets can hold sauces, bread sticks can be arranged in gravy boats and a trifle dish can make a great salad bowl.

FARM
FRESH
August

August

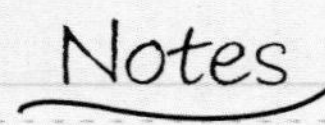

Sunday	Monday	Tuesday
3	4	5
10	11	12
17	18	19
24 / 31	25	26

July

S	M	T	W	T	F	S
		1	2	3	4	5
6	7	8	9	10	11	12
13	14	15	16	17	18	19
20	21	22	23	24	25	26
27	28	29	30	31		

September

S	M	T	W	T	F	S
	1	2	3	4	5	6
7	8	9	10	11	12	13
14	15	16	17	18	19	20
21	22	23	24	25	26	27
28	29	30				

2025

Wednesday	Thursday	Friday	Saturday
		1	2
6	7	8	9
13	14	15	16
20	21	22	23
27	28	29	30

It's difficult to think anything but pleasant thoughts while eating a homegrown tomato.
– Lewis Grizzard

August

Grilled Market Veggies

3 zucchini, sliced 3/4-inch thick
3 yellow squash, sliced 3/4-inch thick
1 baby eggplant, sliced 3/4-inch thick
1 sweet onion, sliced 3/4-inch thick
2 tomatoes, sliced 1-inch thick
1/2 c. balsamic vinegar
1/8 c. canola oil
2 cloves garlic, minced
1 T. fresh rosemary, minced
1 T. fresh oregano, chopped
1 T. fresh basil, chopped
1 T. fresh parsley, minced
1 t. sugar
1/4 t. salt
1/4 t. pepper

Combine vegetables in a large bowl. Whisk together remaining ingredients and pour over vegetables. Toss to coat. Marinate for 30 minutes to one hour. Remove vegetables from marinade with a slotted spoon. Arrange on a grill over medium-hot heat. Grill 2 to 5 minutes on each side, basting often with marinade, until tender. Makes 6 servings.

1 Friday

2 Saturday

3 Sunday

August

Monday 4

Tuesday 5

Wednesday 6

Thursday 7

Friday 8

Saturday 9

Sunday 10

August

11 Monday

12 Tuesday

13 Wednesday

14 Thursday

15 Friday

16 Saturday

17 Sunday

August

Monday 18

Tuesday 19

Wednesday 20

Thursday 21

Friday 22

Saturday 23

Sunday 24

August

25 Monday

26 Tuesday

27 Wednesday

28 Thursday

29 Friday

30 Saturday

31 Sunday

GO TEAM
September

September

Notes

Sunday	Monday	Tuesday
	1 Labor Day	2
7 Grandparents' Day	8	9
14	15	16
21	22 First Day of Autumn Rosh Hashanah (Sundown)	23
28	29	30

August

S	M	T	W	T	F	S
					1	2
3	4	5	6	7	8	9
10	11	12	13	14	15	16
17	18	19	20	21	22	23
24/31	25	26	27	28	29	30

October

S	M	T	W	T	F	S
			1	2	3	4
5	6	7	8	9	10	11
12	13	14	15	16	17	18
19	20	21	22	23	24	25
26	27	28	29	30	31	

2025

Wednesday	Thursday	Friday	Saturday
3	4	5	6
10	11 Patriot Day	12	13
17	18	19	20
24	25	26	27

A good laugh is sunshine in a house.
– William Makepeace Thackeray

September

1 Monday — Labor Day

2 Tuesday

3 

4 

5 Friday

6 Saturday

7 Sunday — Grandparents' Day

September

Monday 8

Tuesday 9

Wednesday 10

Patriot Day

Thursday 11

Friday 12

Saturday 13

Sunday 14

September

15 Monday

16 Tuesday

17 Wednesday

18 Thursday

19 Friday

20 Saturday

21 Sunday

September

First Day of Autumn
Rosh Hashana (Sundown)

Monday 22

Tuesday 23

Wednesday 24

Thursday 25

Friday 26

Saturday 27

Sunday 28

September

29 Monday

30 Tuesday

Hearty Meatball Stew

1 lb. new potatoes, cubed
16-oz. pkg. baby carrots
1 onion, sliced
2 4-oz. cans sliced mushrooms, drained
16-oz. pkg. frozen meatballs
12-oz. jar beef gravy
14-1/2 oz. can Italian-seasoned diced tomatoes
3-1/4 c. water
pepper to taste
14-1/2 oz. can corn, drained

In a large slow cooker, layer all ingredients except corn in the order listed. Cover and cook on low setting for 8 to 10 hours. About one hour before serving, stir in corn. Makes 8 servings.

October

October

Notes

September						
S	M	T	W	T	F	S
	1	2	3	4	5	6
7	8	9	10	11	12	13
14	15	16	17	18	19	20
21	22	23	24	25	26	27
28	29	30				

November						
S	M	T	W	T	F	S
						1
2	3	4	5	6	7	8
9	10	11	12	13	14	15
16	17	18	19	20	21	22
23/30	24	25	26	27	28	29

Crispy air and azure skies,
High above, a white cloud flies,
Bright as newly fallen snow,
Oh, the joy to those who know October!

–Joseph Pullman Porter

Sunday	Monday	Tuesday
5	6	7
12	13 Columbus Day Thanksgiving (Canada)	14
19	20	21
26	27	28

2025

Wednesday	Thursday	Friday	Saturday
1 Yom Kippur (Sundown)	2	3	4
8	9	10	11
15	16	17	18 Sweetest Day
22	23	24	25
29	30	31 Halloween	

October

It's the unexpected touches that make the biggest impression when you are having a party. Don't be afraid to be a little silly at your Halloween bash... a plastic spider on the side of a dessert is sure to bring a smile!

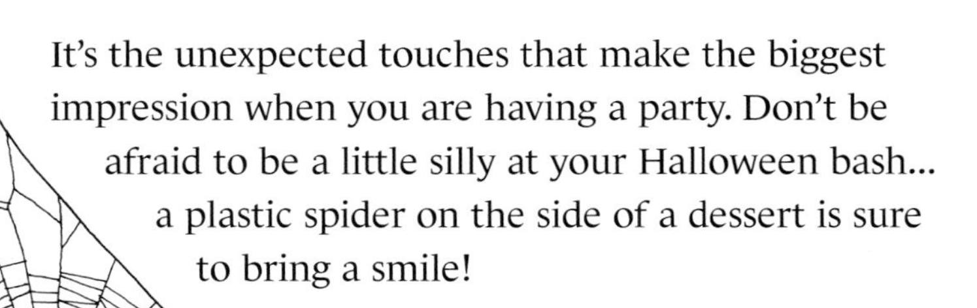

1 Wednesday — Yom Kippur (Sundown)

2 Thursday

3 Friday

4 Saturday

5 Sunday

October

Monday 6

Tuesday 7

Wednesday 8

Thursday 9

Friday 10

Saturday 11

Sunday 12

October

13 Monday — Columbus Day, Thanksgiving (Canada)

14 Tuesday

15 Wednesday

16 Thursday

17 Friday

18 Saturday — Sweetest Day

19 Sunday

October

Monday 20

Tuesday 21

Wednesday 22

Thursday 23

Friday 24

Saturday 25

BOO

Sunday 26

October

27 Monday

28 Tuesday

29 Wednesday

30 Thursday

31 Friday Halloween

November

November

Notes
October
S M T W T F S
1 2 3 4
5 6 7 8 9 10 11
12 13 14 15 16 17 18
19 20 21 22 23 24 25
26 27 28 29 30 31
December
S M T W T F S
1 2 3 4 5 6
7 8 9 10 11 12 13
14 15 16 17 18 19 20
21 22 23 24 25 26 27
28 29 30 31
Sunday
Monday
Tuesday
2
Daylight Savings Ends
3
4
Election Day
9
10
11
Veterans' Day
Remembrance Day
(Canada)
16
17
18
23
30
24
25

2025

Wednesday	Thursday	Friday	Saturday
			1
5	6	7	8
12	13	14	15
19	20	21	22
26	27 Thanksgiving	28	29

It isn't what you have in your pocket that makes you thankful, but what you have in your heart.

– Anonymous

November

Turkey-Vegetable Chowder

This is a hearty chowder made using your leftover turkey!

1/4 c. butter
2 onions, chopped
2 T. all-purpose flour
1 t. curry powder
3 c. chicken broth
1 potato, peeled and chopped
1 c. carrots, peeled and thinly sliced
1 c. celery, thinly sliced
2 T. fresh parsley, minced
1/2 t. dried sage or poultry seasoning
3 c. cooked turkey, chopped
1-1/2 c. half-and-half
10-oz. pkg. frozen chopped spinach
Optional: fresh parsley leaves

Melt butter in a small Dutch oven. Add onions and sauté 10 minutes. Stir in flour and curry powder. Cook 2 minutes. Add broth, potato, carrots, celery, parsley and sage. Reduce heat to low. Cover and simmer 10 to 15 minutes. Add turkey, half-and-half and frozen spinach. Cover and simmer, stirring occasionally, 10 minutes or until heated through. Garnish with fresh parsley leaves, if desired. Makes 8 cups.

1 Saturday

2 Sunday — Daylight Savings Ends

November

Monday 3

Election Day

Tuesday 4

Wednesday 5

Thursday 6

Friday 7

Saturday 8

Sunday 9

November

10 Monday

11 Tuesday

Veterans' Day
Remembrance Day (Canada)

12 Wednesday

13 Thursday

14 Friday

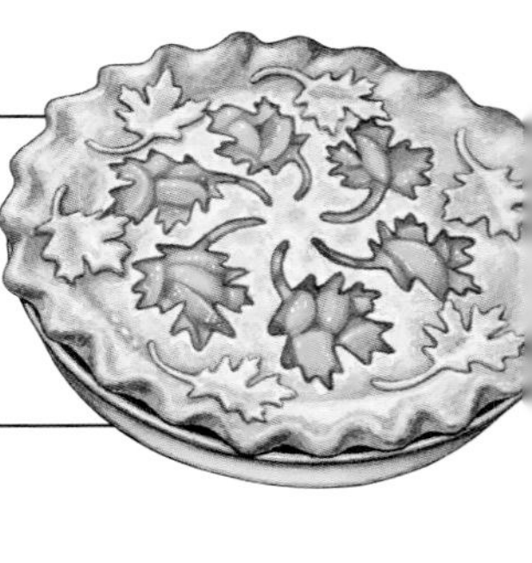

15 Saturday

16 Sunday

November

Monday 17

Tuesday 18

Wednesday 19

Thursday 20

Friday 21

Saturday 22

Sunday 23

November

24 Monday

25 Tuesday

26 Wednesday

27 Thursday Thanksgiving

28 Friday

29 Saturday

30 Sunday

December

December

Notes

Sunday	Monday	Tuesday
	1	2
7	8	9
14 Hanukkah (Sundown)	15	16
21 First Day of Winter	22	23
28	29	30

November

S	M	T	W	T	F	S
						1
2	3	4	5	6	7	8
9	10	11	12	13	14	15
16	17	18	19	20	21	22
23/30	24	25	26	27	28	29

January

S	M	T	W	T	F	S
				1	2	3
4	5	6	7	8	9	10
11	12	13	14	15	16	17
18	19	20	21	22	23	24
25	26	27	28	29	30	31

2025

Wednesday	Thursday	Friday	Saturday
3	4	5	6
10	11	12	13
17	18	19	20
24	25 Christmas	26 Kwanzaa Boxing Day (Canada)	27
31 New Year's Eve			

The holly's up, the house is all bright.
The tree is ready, the candles alight.
Rejoice and be glad, all children tonight!

– Carl Cornelius

December

1 Monday

2 Tuesday

3 Wednesday

4 Thursday

5 Friday

6 Saturday

7 Sunday

December

Monday 8

Tuesday 9

Wednesday 10

Thursday 11

Friday 12

Saturday 13

Hanukkah (Sundown)

Sunday 14

December

15 Monday

16 Tuesday

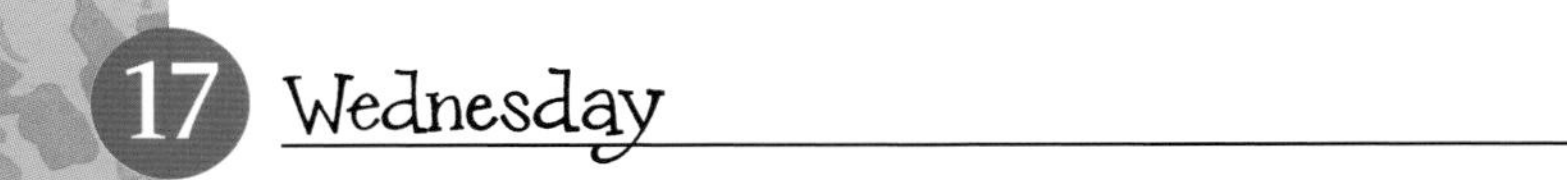

17 Wednesday

18 Thursday

19 Friday

20 Saturday

21 Sunday

First Day of Winter

December

Monday 22

Tuesday 23

Wednesday 24

Christmas

Thursday 25

Kwanzaa
Boxing Day (Canada)

Friday 26

Saturday 27

Sunday 28

December

29 *Monday*

30 *Tuesday*

31 *Wednesday* New Year's Eve

Childhood toys add a feel of nostalgia to Christmas displays. Sailboats, airplanes, teddy bears, dolls and tea sets all bring back fond memories. Set them on tables, stairs, cupboard shelves or mantels.

December

Candy Cane Thumbprints

2/3 c. butter, softened
1/2 c. sugar
1/4 t. salt
1 egg, beaten
1 t. vanilla extract
1-1/2 c. all-purpose flour
Garnish: crushed peppermint candies

With an electric mixer on low speed, blend butter, sugar and salt. Mix in egg and vanilla. Beat in as much flour as possible; stir in remaining flour. Cover; chill for one hour. Shape dough into one-inch balls; place 2 inches apart on ungreased baking sheets. Bake at 375 degrees for 8 to 10 minutes, until lightly golden around edges. Remove from oven; make a thumbprint in each cookie with thumb. Cool. Pipe Filling into centers; sprinkle with crushed candy. Makes about 3 dozen.

Filling:

1/4 c. butter, softened
1/4 t. peppermint extract
1-1/2 c. powdered sugar
2 to 3 t. milk

Blend butter and extract. Gradually add powdered sugar and milk to a piping consistency.

2025

January

S	M	T	W	T	F	S
			1	2	3	4
5	6	7	8	9	10	11
12	13	14	15	16	17	18
19	20	21	22	23	24	25
26	27	28	29	30	31	

February

S	M	T	W	T	F	S
						1
2	3	4	5	6	7	8
9	10	11	12	13	14	15
16	17	18	19	20	21	22
23	24	25	26	27	28	

March

S	M	T	W	T	F	S
						1
2	3	4	5	6	7	8
9	10	11	12	13	14	15
16	17	18	19	20	21	22
23	24	25	26	27	28	29
30	31					

April

S	M	T	W	T	F	S
		1	2	3	4	5
6	7	8	9	10	11	12
13	14	15	16	17	18	19
20	21	22	23	24	25	26
27	28	29	30			

May

S	M	T	W	T	F	S
				1	2	3
4	5	6	7	8	9	10
11	12	13	14	15	16	17
18	19	20	21	22	23	24
25	26	27	28	29	30	31

June

S	M	T	W	T	F	S
1	2	3	4	5	6	7
8	9	10	11	12	13	14
15	16	17	18	19	20	21
22	23	24	25	26	27	28
29	30					

July

S	M	T	W	T	F	S
		1	2	3	4	5
6	7	8	9	10	11	12
13	14	15	16	17	18	19
20	21	22	23	24	25	26
27	28	29	30	31		

August

S	M	T	W	T	F	S
					1	2
3	4	5	6	7	8	9
10	11	12	13	14	15	16
17	18	19	20	21	22	23
24	25	26	27	28	29	30
31						

September

S	M	T	W	T	F	S
	1	2	3	4	5	6
7	8	9	10	11	12	13
14	15	16	17	18	19	20
21	22	23	24	25	26	27
28	29	30				

October

S	M	T	W	T	F	S
			1	2	3	4
5	6	7	8	9	10	11
12	13	14	15	16	17	18
19	20	21	22	23	24	25
26	27	28	29	30	31	

November

S	M	T	W	T	F	S
						1
2	3	4	5	6	7	8
9	10	11	12	13	14	15
16	17	18	19	20	21	22
23	24	25	26	27	28	29
30						

December

S	M	T	W	T	F	S
	1	2	3	4	5	6
7	8	9	10	11	12	13
14	15	16	17	18	19	20
21	22	23	24	25	26	27
28	29	30	31			

2026

January

S	M	T	W	T	F	S
				1	2	3
4	5	6	7	8	9	10
11	12	13	14	15	16	17
18	19	20	21	22	23	24
25	26	27	28	29	30	31

February

S	M	T	W	T	F	S
1	2	3	4	5	6	7
8	9	10	11	12	13	14
15	16	17	18	19	20	21
22	23	24	25	26	27	28

March

S	M	T	W	T	F	S
1	2	3	4	5	6	7
8	9	10	11	12	13	14
15	16	17	18	19	20	21
22	23	24	25	26	27	28
29	30	31				

April

S	M	T	W	T	F	S
			1	2	3	4
5	6	7	8	9	10	11
12	13	14	15	16	17	18
19	20	21	22	23	24	25
26	27	28	29	30		

May

S	M	T	W	T	F	S
					1	2
3	4	5	6	7	8	9
10	11	12	13	14	15	16
17	18	19	20	21	22	23
24	25	26	27	28	29	30
31						

June

S	M	T	W	T	F	S
	1	2	3	4	5	6
7	8	9	10	11	12	13
14	15	16	17	18	19	20
21	22	23	24	25	26	27
28	29	30				

July

S	M	T	W	T	F	S
			1	2	3	4
5	6	7	8	9	10	11
12	13	14	15	16	17	18
19	20	21	22	23	24	25
26	27	28	29	30	31	

August

S	M	T	W	T	F	S
						1
2	3	4	5	6	7	8
9	10	11	12	13	14	15
16	17	18	19	20	21	22
23	24	25	26	27	28	29
30	31					

September

S	M	T	W	T	F	S
		1	2	3	4	5
6	7	8	9	10	11	12
13	14	15	16	17	18	19
20	21	22	23	24	25	26
27	28	29	30			

October

S	M	T	W	T	F	S
				1	2	3
4	5	6	7	8	9	10
11	12	13	14	15	16	17
18	19	20	21	22	23	24
25	26	27	28	29	30	31

November

S	M	T	W	T	F	S
1	2	3	4	5	6	7
8	9	10	11	12	13	14
15	16	17	18	19	20	21
22	23	24	25	26	27	28
29	30					

December

S	M	T	W	T	F	S
		1	2	3	4	5
6	7	8	9	10	11	12
13	14	15	16	17	18	19
20	21	22	23	24	25	26
27	28	29	30	31		

Notes

Notes

Notes

Phone Numbers &
Emergency Contacts

Phone Numbers &
Emergency Contacts

Birthdays & Anniversaries

Birthdays & Anniversaries

Gift List
Gift / Card